Bomb-proof your ....

A Horse's Guide to Teaching Confident Riding

From the stable of
Tina Bettison

www.tinabettison.com

Published by TLB Media Ltd

British Library Cataloguing in Publication Data
A record for this book is available from the British Library

ISBN 978-0-9564506-0-9

Printed and bound in Great Britain
Published by TLB Media Ltd, www.tlbmedia.com

This little book is dedicated to the memory of George, a small dog with a huge personality, who sadly trotted off to doggy heaven as I was finishing this text. He was my muse, my inspiration and a very, very loved companion. He is sorely missed, however his wisdom and his unconditional love will live on.

Message for the Equine Guide

Even the most well seasoned jumpers, dressage queens, show-offs and pleasure riders have at some time or another been faced with a situation or object that is terrifying or confusing. As horses we often just accept that humans will be humans and will lose their marbles every so often. Have human, have incidents! However humans can be trained to cope with any situation and manage the ensuing adrenalin rush. You can teach your human to be confident, obedient and safe whatever you encounter and whatever little challenge you throw at them. This is known as *bomb-proofing* and this little guide should help you take them from quivering wreck to confident rider with these easy -to-use exercises.

How to use this guide

Each 'session' consists of a Thought for Your Human which you should give them as a focus for the week. There are exercise notes for you on the back of each 'thought'. Expect them to read and ponder on their thought daily, but remember that little and often is the best way. Always leave them on a high note! Even if you've only been in session for 15 minutes, and even if it wasn't perfectly executed, when they have done as you asked, leave the lesson there. They have tried and will come to the next lesson so much more willing to learn and with more little cells buzzing in their brains forming the positive and confident connections you want.

Message to your Human

There is nothing worse than feeling the fear and losing your confidence - or wondering if you've ever had any. The good news is that you can build your confidence because you can control your thoughts. With a little equine guidance, the more you think positive thoughts, take positive actions and focus on feeling confident, the more your brain cells will be actively growing confident tendrils. Brain cells that fire together, wire together and the more you fire those cells, the stronger the wiring becomes. That works both ways of course, so make sure you are wiring your brain for confidence rather than lack of it! Here's to your new found confident self!!

Thought for your Human - 1

If I dwell on what I don't want to happen, it is more likely to. I focus on the good things I want from my riding and make them happen instead.

Equine Guidance Notes

Humans have a peculiar habit of worrying more about what hasn't happened – but might have done - than what actually did. They have over-active imaginations that often do not work to their advantage. Whereas we horses respond to whatever *is happening* in this moment, humans respond to *whatever they are thinking about* in this moment which could be something that has never happened at all! Best not dig too deep there, we may open a gargantuan can of worms that we wished we'd left shut. Just get them to focus on what *you* actually want.

Thought for your Human - 2

If we allow anxiety about the past or fear about the
future to command our attention, we often
mess up the present. I will ride in THIS moment.
What is happening NOW is what counts!

Equine Guidance Notes

The key to a confident human is to get them to stay in the present with you. No allowing them to wander off to thoughts of the past or even the future, unless it serves your purpose and you have a completely wicked sense of humour. The merest suggestion of something scary, especially if that spooked them last week, can often be enough to get their attention back to the here and now!

Thought for your Human - 3

My body is a mirror of inner thoughts and beliefs.

Every muscle responds to every thought I think.

My horse feels my every thought: what is in my brain

goes down the reins!

Equine Guidance Notes

If you are a highly strung, nervous horse who seeks confidence from his rider, try not to get a similarly highly strung, confidence seeking, nervous human. You'll both spend all your time together quivering at the back of the stable. References and a thorough vetting are vital to check out your human's compatibility. And don't take on a nervous human just because you feel sorry for them; it won't work and there'll be tears at bedtime.

A what if.... thought can be a positive thought too.
I wonder what will happen when I change my
what if...worries to what if... I get what I want?

Equine Guidance Notes

A smart quick thinking human can be harder to train but their warp speed brain may be quite handy if you enjoy certain disciplines which require a rapid response to your decision making, such as spooking at speed or dancing the Quick Step with a falling leaf as you enter the arena at A. Do not allow your human to make their own decisions – you are the expert in avoidance of scary monsters, they should always defer to you.

Thought for your Human - 5

I have the power to make the changes I want in my riding. I might need guidance, I might need motivation, but I can do it if I focus on what I want to achieve.

Equine Guidance Notes

If you have a human that has been previously well trained, possesses a quiet attitude, a general acceptance of whatever you ask of them and mild curiosity, without thinking too much, then you are onto a winner. This one will be eminently bomb-proof-able, but probably as rare as rocking horse s**t. However they do exist so never give up hope that one day you will be united with The One. In the meantime, gentle guidance and the odd sugar lump for motivation will help you pass the time with the human you've got.

Thought for your Human - 6

I let go of past negative experiences. I do not use
yesterday's difficulties to create today's experiences.
I create fresh new thoughts to achieve my goals.

Equine Guidance Notes

Does your human have good manners? Do they stand quietly while you are grooming them? Do they flinch when you stand on their toe? Do they recoil when you wave your hooves near their face? Don't despair if your human is uneducated. They may just have had some poor training by a previous owner and their heart may still be in the right place. You can bomb-proof them, it might just take a little longer and a little more patience.

Thought for your Human - 7

When I am not quite getting what I want in my riding I will look for alternative creative ideas rather than dwelling on the cause.

Equine Guidance Notes

It is vital to know and understand your human's history. Clearly if they have had some negative past experiences, particularly around horses, then you need to take account of this in your training, and more patience or therapy may be needed. Avoid taking on a human whose history is a complete unknown; it's hard to assess and manage their difficult behaviour when you don't know the roots of its cause.

Thought for your Human - 8

If we allow them their way, our fears have a powerful
influence over our thoughts, feelings and actions.
If my fears were a caged bird, would I keep them
locked inside or set them free to fly away?

Equine Guidance Notes

Although we shouldn't make a big thing about the gender of your human, it is a contributing factor you should consider in your assessment as they deal with fear differently. Females of the species tend to be more herd-bound, can be moody especially when in season, and (particularly when in season) are more scatty and flighty than the male. Males are often more focused, gung-ho and confident, but are also more opinionated and aggressive, which can lead to argument. You will need different strategies for dealing with each.

Thought for your Human - 9

If my horse could hear all my thoughts, would he
want to listen or would he put his hooves over his ears?
Supposing I just allow only the thoughts into my head
that he would be happy to hear?

Equine Guidance Notes

How well can you read your human and hear their thoughts? When they 'blow up', did you sense it coming or was it a complete surprise? You may be adept at recognizing a muscle twitch in the herd, but do you know your human muscle twitches? Can you pick up the wobbly lip, the teary ears, the bodily tension of frustration versus the rigor mortis of abject terror? The better you are at picking up these subtle signals, the easier you will find it to bomb-proof your human.

Thought for your Human - 10

Sometimes if we aren't getting the right answer,
it's because we aren't asking the right question.
If my horse isn't responding how I want, do I need to
ask a him different question or put it another way?

Equine Guidance Notes

Sometimes your human just won't understand what you are asking for. Be patient, they are only human after all. It may help to pose the question in a different way. For example - if they don't understand that your taking out the electric fencing for the fifth time that week means that you wish to sample the greener grass on the other side, removing the posts one by one with your teeth should help them get the idea that there is more than one way to communicate a desired outcome.

Thought for your Human - 11

A definition of insanity is to keep doing the same thing and expecting a different result. If I keep doing what I've always done, I will get the result I have always got. Is it the result I want?

Equine Guidance Notes

If your human is of a particularly nervous disposition, a little jog sideways every so often, accompanied by cocking your head suspiciously at the hedge for no apparent reason will keep them on the alert. A mere plastic bag-induced tiny spook will then be enough to make their heart stop. Repeat frequently until your human ceases to react and chooses a different response.

Thought for your Human - 12

Comparing myself to others will hinder rather than help. Emulating someone I admire, thinking the way they think and imagining myself riding as they ride, will stimulate me to reach towards their level.

Equine Guidance Notes

Modeling master bomb-proofers is a great way to improve your skills. Here's an example from the doyenne of human trainers. Do not alert your human, it ruins the exercise. When you spot something scary (a large tractor will do), spin towards the ditch and plunge deftly into it. Execute a turn on the haunches and scrabble back out. Judge the speed of oncoming traffic to ensure it is slowing down, though this exercise does help drivers practice their emergency stop. Just check your human is still up there and breathing before walking on as though nothing had happened.

Contentment stems from peace of mind. If I am
anxious or upset, how can my horse be contented?
To still my mind I'll walk with him quietly and
think of how fortunate I am to be doing something
I love, spending time with the horse I love.
I wonder how contented could we both be?

Equine Guidance Notes

A gentle exercise to start off a nervous human in their spook-proofing is the suspended spook. Cantering along happily and rhythmically, you just hold your breath and suspend yourself for a split second above the ground, before exhaling, returning to earth and cantering on. Your human will probably giggle nervously and wonder what happened, but after a few repetitions they will soon be used to it and may even find it fun.

What is my primary riding goal? What step will I take in the next 7 days to reinforce my commitment to that goal?

Equine Guidance Notes

There are always going to be objects that humans want to avoid; for example plastic bags in hedges, wheelie bins, flapping things, balloons on gates, cows, sheep, show jumps in the corner of the school, buckets, chairs… the list is endless. Set little goals to address one of these issues per week and you'll soon have them nailed and your human de-sensitised to them. At first you may have to ignore your human adopting the foetal position and grasping your mane so hard it comes out in clumps. Sometimes you have to endure a little pain for their gain.

Thought for your Human - 15

Bad habits are often difficult to overcome because they feel right. A dropped shoulder, a collapsed hip or a negative thought can feel so right, but be so wrong. What are my bad habits? Which one will I change into a good habit this week?

Equine Guidance Notes

Sometimes you will have to deal with the physical habits of humans which don't help in the confidence-building process. A human who spends all day sitting hunched over a computer is not going to be well balanced in the saddle without a great deal of practice. Do not under any circumstances start compensating for their misalignment - no point in both of you having back-ache. No, let them wobble and fall off as much as necessary until they get the message that a visit to the chiropractor might be a good thing.

Thought for your Human - 16

True harmony in riding is a balance of the
physiological (body), intellectual (mind) and
psychological (spirit) for both horse and rider.
How balanced is my riding? Am I developing
myself and my horse in all three areas?

Equine Guidance Notes

Your human needs to learn balance, trust and confidence on all levels: physical, psychological and intellectual. Teach them this by the toss and catch method. Firstly send them flying when you spook sideways – flying away from you and out of the saddle. It might serve your purpose to lose them a couple of times to get them desensitised to that possibility. The second part of this exercise is to throw them upwards in a controlled movement so you can come back underneath and catch them again. This builds trust and confidence that you are in fact a safe pair of hooves.

Thought for your Human - 17

'Be the change you want to see in your horse'
If I want my horse to be calmer, I become calmer
in myself. If I want my horse to be more supple,
flexible and softer, I become more supple, flexible
and softer in myself.

Equine Guidance Notes

Take a leaf from Mahatma Ghandi who said 'Be the change you want to see in the world'. Sometimes you will have to lead the way and be the change you'd like to see in your human. Practise equine yoga and aerobics (otherwise known as rolling and 'airs above the ground') for calming, suppleness and flexibility so you can teach these qualities to your human.

Thought for your Human - 18

The greatest teacher I will ever have is my horse.

His feedback will always be honest and immediate.

He has no agenda beyond his survival and wellbeing.

What have I learned from my horse this week?

Equine Guidance Notes

Humour is a vital teaching aid and helps your human learn more easily. For example, letting yourself out of your stable will bring a smile to their face. Head for a juicy bit of grass. So much the better if it is their well kept lawn – always full of nutrients – and has a laser alarm across it to alert your human to intruders. Wandering back and forth across the alarm at 3am will certainly get them giggling, especially when they're running about the garden, half asleep, in their pyjamas, brandishing a baseball bat, looking for burglars.

Thought for your Human - 19

Tension and worry in my mind transforms into
tension and stiffness in my body. Where do I hold
my tension? This week I will practise 'letting go'
in my mind and in my body.

Equine Guidance Notes

Worried and anxious humans will be tense and stiff in their body as well as their mind. Help them to let go, relax and shake out their tensions by taking them for a smart and bouncy working trot down a rutty bridle path.

Thought for your Human - 20

If I have any thought in my mind other than where I want my horse to place his next footfall, then I am not in the present, and I am not 'present' with my horse. Therefore I am leaving the moment to moment decisions to him. He really doesn't want this responsibility.

Equine Guidance Notes

Building your human's confidence in any situation is an important part of your teaching role. A cross country course is great confidence building territory, but any schooling area will do. Lull your human into a sense of false security by pretending to aim directly at the fence, and then just dip out at the last moment; it's much more fun when they aren't expecting it and will give them confidence for those situations when you make an unplanned, last-minute run-out decision.

I don't have to deal with my fears alone.

Asking for help is a sign of strength.

Who can I ask for help and support this week?

Equine Guidance Notes

How is the journey so far? Do you love being around humans and can you take their idiosyncrasies in your stride? Can you keep your head while your human is losing theirs? Your human will reflect your emotions. Can you stay in the present moment and take the leadership role? Don't worry if you are uncertain and don't be afraid to ask your herd mentor to help you build your own positive experiences as you continue your training sessions with your human.

Thought for your Human - 22.

This week I will write down all the positive and fabulous experiences I have had with my horse to refer to when I get wobbly moments.

Since humans have this strange ability to mostly remember the bad experiences, encourage them with some good ones. Sharing your carrots with them, softly grooming behind their ears, putting your head on their shoulder for hugs and teaching them little tricks should give them something positive to add to their gratitude journal..

If my horse is doing something I am not happy with,
what is he trying to communicate? My focus for
this week is to listen to my horse.

Equine Guidance Notes

The meaning of communication is the response you get, so if you are not getting the desired response from your human, you may have to adjust your communication. For example if the nervous whinny and small shudder isn't getting through, try a louder whinny with the planted feet approach. And if that doesn't work, you'll have to resort to the fire-breathing snort accompanied by an elevated piaffe/passage.

The best way to build my confidence is in small steps,

taken slowly. What small step can I take this week?

Equine Guidance Notes

Take a leaf from police horses who are masters at training humans. Whatever new obstacle they face, from fluttering flags to fire hoops, they introduce the challenge to their human slowly and from a distance. Gradually they bring it closer to the human and repeat the exercise until the human can face it without so much as a flick of the ear. Reward plays an important role too. Always encourage your human to carry mints so you can reward yourself for a job well done.

Thought for your Human - 25

I don't have to achieve everything all at once - nor do I
have to 'do' anything. It's ok to take my time,
to have fun and to say 'no, that's not for me'.

Equine Guidance Notes

And finally, if it isn't fun, don't do it. Working with humans should be fun, first and foremost. There is no point in forcing yourself or your human to do something you don't enjoy - even for the sake of bomb-proofing. If you have to plant your feet and put your hooves on your hips to reinforce the 'no', do it. When your human has stopped flapping at your insolence, they'll be grateful for your confident decision.